WE ARE THE YOUTH OF THE NATION

Brittany Simon

Order this book online at www.trafford.com/08-1213
or email orders@trafford.com

Most Trafford titles are also available at major online book retailers.

My editor: Katie Gutierrez of Legacy Editorial Consulting

Note for Librarians: A cataloguing record for this book is available from Library and Archives Canada at www.collectionscanada.ca/amicus/index-e.html

ISBN: 978-1-4251-8710-1

We at Trafford believe that it is the responsibility of us all, as both individuals and corporations, to make choices that are environmentally and socially sound. You, in turn, are supporting this responsible conduct each time you purchase a Trafford book, or make use of our publishing services. To find out how you are helping, please visit www.trafford.com/responsiblepublishing.html

Our mission is to efficiently provide the world's finest, most comprehensive book publishing service, enabling every author to experience success. To find out how to publish your book, your way, and have it available worldwide, visit us online at www.trafford.com/10510

www.trafford.com

North America & international
toll-free: 1 888 232 4444 (USA & Canada)
phone: 250 383 6864 ♦ fax: 250 383 6804
email: info@trafford.com

The United Kingdom & Europe
phone: +44 (0)1865 487 395 ♦ local rate: 0845 230 9601
facsimile: +44 (0)1865 481 507 ♦ email: info.uk@trafford.com

10 9 8 7 6 5 4 3 2

A Note from the Author

What you are about to read is a take on the world from how I see it. While most of the statements in this book are my opinions, those that are fact are stated as such. Additionally, all of the comments from the youth are authentic and were submitted to me via my website. I want to thank everyone who wrote in; you are the future generations of America who will make the most difference in our world.

THIS BOOK IS DEDICATED TO AMERICA.

"I pledge allegiance to the flag of the United States of America, and to the Republic for which it stands. One nation under God, indivisible, with liberty and justice for all."

- The Pledge of Allegiance (incase you forgot)

CAUGHT

Young I may be
But sheltered I am not
I live in a battle
In which I am caught.

Take a line of delusion
Straight through your nose
Making you numb
From your head to your toes.

Wake up tomorrow
Not remembering today
The youth is what they are targeting
They're feasting on easy prey.

So
Young I may be
But sheltered I am not
I live in a battle
In which I am caught.

- Bria Hampton, 15, Iowa

FOREWORD

I am nineteen and just a child. This child, however, has seen sorrow, death, love, and courage. I am the daughter of immigrant parents who struggled to come to this country from the Middle East and raise me as best they could. I have seen my older brothers leave home to serve in the military and fight a war. I have felt what it is like to love, because I love my parents and nine siblings more than anything in this world. And I know what it is like to watch death eat away a loved one before my eyes. All these things I have seen, and yet I have so much more to experience.

I began this project because I want to experience so much more throughout my life—but how can I experience anything when all I can think about is how my country is dying? I feel as though I can't enjoy life until I have made things right, until I help fix my country's ailments. My country and my way of life are *my* passion, and I will not let them be taken from me without a fight. I will never give up, and I will never give in. I know I'm a part of a future group of generations that will bring back the principles and morals upon which America was built.

At one point—it may be now—there will be a line, and we'll all have to choose a side to join. One wins and one fails; there is no third choice.

Which side will you be on?

The purpose of this project is to make people aware that the youth of America are smarter than they are perceived. This book is a collage of comments from that youth—including myself–and each chapter begins with my personal beliefs on a topic greatly affecting our country. Perhaps more importantly, however, within the following chapters, you'll see unedited e-mails from youth around the country who felt compelled to share their opinions on the big issues. I'm very proud of every single comment sent to me, whether it coincides with my beliefs or not. Just the fact that my peers messaged me is sign enough that we, the youth of America, are strong, bold, and unafraid.

Chapter One

AMERICAN PRIDE

"If you're going to burn the flag, wrap it around yourself first."
– Unknown

My maternal grandfather was a father to seventeen children, not counting the miscarriages. He married my grandmother when he was eighteen and she was twelve. My grandmother was fourteen when she had her first child, and my grandparents own a brick home in Elqosh, Iraq that has been in the family for hundreds of years.

So, imagine my mother's footsteps. Imagine being a seven-year-old girl who is the fourteenth child of seventeen.

You enter through the main wooden doors of your home and end up in a courtyard. You see your family members gathered around—your father, mother and siblings, your grandparents and your uncle's family all living together in one home.

The cellar door is to your right, and will lead you to where the hay is kept. It's also where a single bowl and bucket rest, waiting for the next family member to bathe. You have to be very careful not to waste any water as you do, though; you only get this privilege once a week. The only water supply comes from the rain or a neighbor's well, and water is scarce and so precious that not even a drop can go without use.

In addition to being a place of hygiene, the cellar is also where your parents hide you when the Muslim soldiers come searching for the men in your village. The soldiers come into the village at random and always in groups. Your family is targeted more than others because your father is one of the men who refuse to join the Muslims' political party. The Muslims have many organizations, all corrupt and dangerous, but no matter how much they threaten, your father will not be swayed.

When the men are away, the women are the sole protectors, and in the Middle East that is a joke. But your family holds on to faith and hope to get them through these times.

Your nose wrinkles as you look at the cellar door. You hate being crammed in there with all your siblings when the soldiers come into the city. Your toes wiggle almost automatically as you imagine the cold floor, the dirt between your toes, and the snakes and black widows hiding in the corners.

You shake your head and, with each turn, the memories depart, leaving only a smile for your family before you walk inside the house and past the three bedrooms. Each room houses an entire family, no matter how large that family becomes. Next, you walk up the stairs and onto the roof. The roof is flat, and in the summertime you and your family sleep on top of it, desperate for a chance breeze. This is your home.

On a normal day in Iraq, you wake up early and go to school and church before completing chores, which consist of collecting water, food, hay, and anything else that can be used for survival. There is no running water, no toilet paper, no television, no stove, and no electricity. During the day, it's your job to walk along the roadside with a bucket in your hand and scoop up all the cow manure to use as firewood.

At around three in the afternoon comes dinnertime. You see what your grandmother has made you, and your wrinkle your nose: another day-old meal of mostly rice. You eat the spoiled food, and the sour taste will stick to your tongue for years to come.

When the sun sets, you don't wander out of the house by yourself, and if you do, the only light you have comes from the moon. Though the crime rate is low in the village, it doesn't mean that you're always safe. Domestic fights break out among the villagers and sometimes result in death. And then there's the fear of snakes and deadly insects.

Now, imagine some time passes and your father is once again on the run. This is normal for your family; your father is a very wanted man because he will not conform to the Muslim ways. As a strong Chaldean Catholic, he holds fast to his faith and will bend for no one. Being a Chaldean is more then just an ethnicity; it's a way of life. The Muslims wish to convert him to their side, be it through verbal persuasion or force. But your father knows that they commit murder and rape, and control the weak through brutality. So he hides in the mountains and sneaks visits to his family every few months, whenever he can.

This is the life my mother experienced until she was nine and finally able to fly to America through Ellis Island, New York. When they arrived, her mother walked around with a sign around her neck that read: "I don't speak English, help me get to the next terminal." My mother was with five of her siblings, and she still remembers the crowds of people that were kind enough to help them get to their destination. Two years of separation later, she was finally reunited with her father and older siblings.

My father's story is one that is equally important to tell, but I can only give you a taste of what it was like to be him. My father was one of eight children. His oldest brother was drafted into the Iraqi army, even though he didn't want anything to do with it. As my father approached adult age, when he could be drafted at any time, my grandfather took a stand and said that that was enough. He moved his family to America because he couldn't stand to see any more of his children drafted into the corrupt Muslim world. My father came to America when he was seventeen years old, and he struggled to learn English while dedicating himself to his studies. Through patience, time, and experience he became an electrical engineer. He has been in business for twelve years building high-speed continuous motion assembly machines for a vast number of industries, such as plastics, pharmaceuticals, hardware, automatic, food, chemicals, and electronics.

Everything my parents experienced contributed to the way they raised me. First and foremost, my parents raised me to be a patriot. They only spoke English at home and have refused to teach me their native language because they want me to fully love what I am: an American. Through blood I am Middle Eastern, but only in blood. In spirit and through birth and my upbringing, I am an American. My parents don't really have any good memories of their country or childhoods. Civilizations change, and the Chaldean people are no longer the strong Catholics they were hundreds of years ago; many of them speak Arabic and even mix their culture with the Arab culture and call it Chaldean.

Despite their reservations with certain parts of their culture, I was never deprived of others. My mother taught me how to belly dance, and my father sings and plays Middle Eastern music constantly. Both of my parents are excellent cooks, and we eat Chaldean food, like rice, tomato past based soup and stuffed grape leaves, almost everyday. I never felt like I was missing anything, and I still don't.

Now that you know my family's history, I would like to welcome you into the world as I see it.

I would like you think back to 9/11. Do you remember what

you were doing on the day of that horrific attack? What did you do when you heard the news? I prayed three rosaries, though at the time I was very young and thought it tedious.

Well, imagine your alarm clock goes off that morning, but you ignore it. Just this once, you tell yourself, you'll sleep in. You fall asleep. You wake up at noon and turn on the television, and your country is in catastrophic disarray.

Your eyes open wide, your jaw drops, and your hands begin to shake. You ask yourself so many questions, all consisting of the same theme: *How did this happen? When? Who could have done it? Is this a dream?*

It only took one day for a rage of emotions to erupt from America. We came together as one; no individual cared about political affiliations, religion, or anything except that our people were hurt. Thousands of firefighters took leaves of absence to help in New York, as did volunteer policemen, priests, and other workers. Afterward, the American people exploded with passionate vows of retribution for the 3,000 people killed that day. And, of course, many stewed with racial hatred for the Muslims–an important topic I will hit upon later.

After 9/11, American pride consumed the nation. Then, after a while, it began to die. Slowly, those who were so patriotic when the towers fell began to fade back into the dark. And the people who were my age and younger at the time of the attacks seemed to forget the horror.

Today, you walk through a high school campus and students are wearing other countries' colors, Nazi logos, or shirts mocking America. In those campuses, you hear a lot about brown pride, gay pride, black pride, but whatever happened to *American* pride? When I was in high school in a very low crime, country town, I saw a lot of "brown pride" stickers, colors, and messages written along the walls and bathroom stalls. That saying has created a permanent stain in my memory, because most of the kids who represented it were pro-illegal immigrants in this country.

One might argue that the American government is trying to stop immigrants from coming here, so why shouldn't these students feel resentful? But the truth is that the American government isn't trying to stop immigrants from coming here; my relatives have immigrated and are still immigrating here. Rather, the American government is trying to stop *illegal* immigrants from crossing our borders. You may think it's heartless and cruel not to let people who are suffering have a better life, but again I remind you of my mother's story.

I can't say enough that it will take you and me to make a difference in our society. I implore you to read about your country, learn about her and what she is. Find out why people say she's the best, why she is the "Land of the Free." Go out and vote, become informed. Don't just go off of what CNN or Fox News reports.

Stand and face the flag when the Pledge of Allegiance is being said. Smile when you see a member of the military. Don't give a cold shoulder to the men and woman in uniform because you disagree with the war. The military is comprised of people doing their jobs, just like you and me.

Don't hold war protests that do more harm than good. Don't masquerade as the honored men and women who have died for you and this country. People that do these things are not patriots; they don't care about the military. They are selfish bigots with nothing to live for.

Is there no more respect?

I am an eighteen-year-old kid, an adult according to the legal suits, and I can recognize disrespect when I see it. People call it free speech; I call it vile retribution for something they brought upon themselves.

Have some pride.

Take a little and give a lot.

From the Youth: messages sent via email.

I may not agree with everything that the President is standing for, but I do know this: We are lucky. So incredibly lucky. We are relatively safe. Compared with the Middle East we live in heaven. They would kill to live like us. We need to stop whining about what we don't have and start showing some gratitude for what we DO have.

-Brittany, 14, New Hampshire.

As a Bible College graduate and a teacher in my church, more than anything else, I cannot stand the statement that "America is a Christian nation." I don't want to talk about the founding fathers or whether or not America was supposed to be the next Promised Land. What I want to say is that the term Christian defines a person who has surrendered their life to follow the Jesus Christ of the Bible. It could be debated whether or not a nation could ever be defined as Christian, but if it is possible, I will say that the term does not define America today.

America has always held the promise (and I pray will always continue to hold the promise) of freedom of religion. But this idea of separation of church and state has been pushed too far the wrong way. The first amendment of the Bill of Rights says, "Congress shall make no law respecting an establishment of religion, or prohibiting the free exercise thereof," yet what we see continually happening is that this is taken to mean freedom from religion, rather than freedom of religion. No matter [what] your personal beliefs are, the reality is that any government intending to work for the betterment of its people must always have an overarching moral code which it will stand on.

Aristotle said, "Tolerance and apathy are the last virtues of a dying society," yet it seems that these two precisely describe modern day America. We have come to a place where no one wants to buy into absolute truths, yet we still expect that America can hold on to her freedoms and privileges without question. If we no longer hold to any self-evident truths, then we have no grounds on which our nation can stand.

If the moral standard for America is to take all you can before it is taken from you, then we do not believe "that all men are created equal" nor do all men share in the rights of "life, liberty and the pursuit of happiness." What we essentially believe is that I have the right to do whatever I want even at the expense of everyone else around. And then when I feel that my self-given rights are violated I loudly declare intolerance.

If America is to remain great, we must once again stand on a solid moral code in which my rights and your rights are respected equally no matter race, age, gender, or religion. We must become one nation still promising liberty and justice for all, not just for the one who complains the loudest. What this must mean is that tolerance is not always a virtue; equality is. For equality to continue, certain things cannot be tolerated. I will not declare that America must become a great Christian nation once again. But if America will not hold firm to the moral fabric that founded this nation, then we will surely cease to exist. Great men and women have shown great intolerance to protect the freedoms we hold so dear. If we do not continue to claim these freedoms for ourselves, then our apathy will surely lead us to destruction.

-Scott Ingram, 23, Texas

Chapter Two

POLITICAL RAMPAGE: THE WAR ON TERROR

"We make war that we may live in peace."
- Aristotle 325 B.C.

In 1981, Ronald Reagan addressed the youth with the following statement: "We need you; we need your youth, your strength, and your idealism, to help us make right what is wrong."

Reagan's quote expresses the importance of being a youth willing to take action. I'm not saying that America's youth have all the answers, but I do feel that the youth can sometimes see the truth like they see the sun: glaring and obvious. Yet, there are adults who deny that the sun even exists. It boggles my mind when I hear people in power deny the truth, even if the proof is staring them straight in the eye. I always think of the people who truly believe that the Holocaust never occurred. I mean, come on!

Now, there was a time in our history when the youth did take action and it turned out to be, for the most part, horrifying. The best example I can think of is Kent State.

During the Vietnam War, the youth of America dove into what they believed to be the liberation movement. The youth, mostly college students, protested sending their fellow Americans into a war zone.

The following are very different descriptions of the same event:

The Kent State protest was inspired after Richard Nixon's election in 1968. He promised to end the war, but in 1969 the My Lai Massacre was exposed. The massacre was the mass murder, conducted by the U.S. Army, of the unarmed citizens of the Republic of Vietnam. It occurred on March 16, 1968, and the majority of the victims were women and children.

That alone rocked America to the core. Then, the following month, the American people saw the first draft lottery since World War II. Various youth groups gathered outside Kent State University in Kent, Ohio for a heated protest; some for fear of being drafted and others against the American invasion of Cambodia. The youth groups and students came together in vast numbers, despite the work of the university leaders who tried to cancel the event. Students attacked police officers after the police gave fair warning, and the police reacted with tear gas and force after students refused to comply. Four students were killed and nine others wounded, and the tragic event served to further divide America across political lines. Indeed, people still argue about what happened that day.

In the movies, Hollywood tends to focus on the struggle and hurt that the youth experienced during the Kent State shootings. The movies always make the police and the government the enemy. But in reality, the Vietnam-Kent State protest was anything but peaceful. So who was wrong? For some of us, the Kent State shootings represent death, chaos, and a time of true sadness. For others, the events represent free speech, righteous rebellion, and a time to belong to something, to be someone.

I believe that the youth of the sixties were incredibly confused. They wanted to stop the killing, but to stop the killing they had to kill. To end a war, people have to die. The youth did what they could: they retaliated, they rebelled, and they became known as the youth who liberated America.

Fast forward to today. As I've discussed, I am the first generation of my family to be born in America. My parents emigrated from Iraq to flee the persecution of the Iraqi government in the 1960s. It took my mother's family twelve years before they could live in the U.S. legally. I know that, for some, it just sounds like a good Hollywood story of a struggling family, but it was a horrifying truth for mine, and the current War on Terror affects my family extensively. We still have relatives in Iraq who will not leave their birthplace, even with the war all around them. They are waiting for the American government to give them a country in which they can live peacefully.

America prides herself in being the best, and she is that; never doubt it. But America does have some faults—like her people, for one thing. Don't get offended; I'm only speaking the truth. We are a jumbled sort of people. We want this and that, but we don't take the time to vote, and then we complain when something doesn't go our way.

I constantly hear people saying that we should pull out of this war, that we only went there for oil. I don't believe that at all. I truly believe the Muslim radicals have weapons of mass destruction. My uncle told me that when he was a part of the Iraqi army, the solders of higher rank would blindfold him and take him underground to secret bases of operation. They didn't want him to know where he was going in case he ever betrayed them. They took him down to a bunker underground and when they unblended him there were explosives as far as the eye could see. These people aren't stupid, or our job in the Middle East would have been completed years ago.

Every move that we make in this war affects a multitude of things; the issues are all interconnected. For example, there is no such thing as, "We're talking about abortion, so stick to the topic," because abortion ties into things like women's rights and stem cell research. In the same vein, the War on Terror affects soldiers' rights; whether or not the American people even want to go to war; the lives of thousands and thousands of Iraqis, Americans, and Muslims; economy; and civil rights, just to name a few. The war affects our ailing economy; gas prices are shooting through the roof, and it's getting harder to sell homes. This war affects everyone; it's bigger than just you and me.

I came across this quote by Ernest Hemingway and I think it says it well: "Once we have a war there is only one thing to do. It must be won. For defeat brings worse things than any that can ever happen in war."

My point is that war isn't pretty, easy, or wanted by anyone. I want to bring our troops home, too, but I know we can't until this war is done. America does not invade countries for domination, but for protection or out of defense. We need to sit back and remember that we are in this war to help people who can't help themselves. We are in this war because of a threat that killed almost three thousands of our citizens.

Now, I would like you to imagine what it would be like to not listen to the radio for one week and neither watch television nor read newspapers. In other words, you cut yourself off from all media outlets. You would probably go about your days unaware that there was even a war going on. Because of our efficient military leaders and our volunteer military, we have freedom. Because of our armed forces, we even have the freedom to (ignorantly) protest what they're doing, if we're so inclined. We have the freedom to destroy this country from the inside out. We have the freedom to worry about taking our dogs to the vet, making sure our gray hair is dyed, and making sure our clothes are pressed to perfection.

Because of our soldiers and our president, 9/11 was the last attack that the terrorists were able to carry out on our home soil.

I believe that we have the best military in the world. I support the boots on the ground while they fight for me. I received a forward on MySpace and would like to share it with you now. I think it confirms my trust in our military and proves that we are always five steps ahead. I'm sorry to say I don't know who wrote it, but I thank whoever did.

The Aisle Seat

Two Radical Arab Terrorists boarded a flight out
of London.

One
took a window seat and the other sat next to him
in the middle seat...
Just before takeoff, a U.S.

Marine sat down in the
aisle seat.

After
take off, the Marine kicked his shoes off, wiggled
his toes and was
settling in when the Arab in the window seat said:
"I need to get up and get a coke."

"Don't get up,"
said the Marine, "I'm in the aisle
seat, I'll get it for you."

As soon as he left, one of the Arabs picked up
the Marine's shoe and
spat in it.

When the Marine returned with the
coke, the other Arab
said, "That looks good, I'd really like
one, too."

Again, the Marine
obligingly went to fetch it.

While he was gone the
other Arab picked up
the Marine's other shoe and spat in it.

When the
Marine returned, they
all sat back and enjoyed the flight.

As the plane was landing, the Marine slipped his
feet into his shoes
and knew immediately what had happened.

He leaned
over and asked his
Arab neighbors...

"Why does it have to be this
way? How long must
this go on? This fighting between our nations?
This hatred? This

animosity? This spitting in shoes and pissing in cokes?"

THE FEW.

THE PROUD.

THE MARINES

My second oldest brother, Michael, was an army soldier for more than five years and served two tours in Iraq. He signed up for the military when he was seventeen, in August of 2001, one month before 9/11. The day he came home in his uniform was one of the proudest moments in my family's history. My oldest brother, David, is a Marine. David has served two tours in Iraq and one tour in Okinawa, Japan.

The military is more than just a job to my family. These military soldiers are the ones who deserve millions of dollars for what they do, not the movie stars. Every time I see any man or woman in uniform, my heart skips a beat and a smile spreads across my face before I even have time to blink. I feel a pull to all people in uniform because I know what they do for this country. And even if some of those soldiers don't know how important they are to society, it's okay because *I* know, and I will never forget what they did and do for this country and our way of life every day of their service.

Those who don't feel the same about the war and the military often argue that Afghanistan attacked us and Saddam didn't. But I have an analogy for you.

Imagine that you decide to clean one of the dressers in your room. "That's it," you tell yourself. You start cleaning behind your dresser and see that the mess trails to the dresser next to that and then under the bed. You aren't going to ignore the cobwebs, old food, and sour smell that's coming from those places, are you? You're going to clean it all up, even if your original goal was only to clean the first dresser.

That's how I see this war. I want our troops to come home, but we can't do that until we finish the job. We can't go into a war zone and ignore the other terrorists there just because initially we said we wanted Bin Laden and not Saddam. But my family was persecuted under the rule of Saddam, and he was just like Hitler, just like Bin Laden; all these men are the same. They all wanted power, control, and the deaths of those who defied them. The only way they differ is in their choice of weapons.

From the Youth:

I would like to start off the comments with one from my second oldest brother, who served in the Army and performed two tours in Iraq:

<u>Reaction time</u>

TRUE STORY: An airborne soldier was in a plane flying toward the drop zone. After 30 minutes, the Jump Master gave the two minuet signal. The soldier stood and got himself prepared. 60 seconds....30 seconds....10 seconds.... Green Light. One after another his platoon leaped from the plane out into darkness. He stepped to the door and jumped. It felt like being sucked into a vacuum. Four long seconds passed before his shute opened. When it did he felt a tug at his left leg. In the moonlight he could make out a suspension line of another parachute wrapped around his leg. Looking down further he saw another soldier about ten feet below him

"Get loose!" the other soldier yelled up.

Pulling and yanking to no avail he called down "I can't!"

"Then climb down!" came the response.

Pulling up on the suspension line to lower himself down was all that was needed to get free. With a snap the line broke and the two parachutes went in opposite directions. The soldier had just enough time to pull the release cord of his rucksack, attached to a 15 foot cord, before he hit the ground. With the wind knocked out of him he wondered how he made it down without at least one broken bone. He laid there for a good ten minuets, just breathing, with his chute fluttering in the wind.

A military jump on average is from about 1200 feet in the air. This soldier jumped at 1000. 4 seconds waiting for the chute to open put him at about 450-550 feet. About 50 seconds to fall the rest after your shute opens. So everything mentioned above happened in about 45 seconds. Pretty good reaction time I'd say.

Many thoughts race through a person's head when faced with extraordinary circumstances. Everyone has a reaction time. Whether it's a combat veteran or a parent or even a Good Samaritan, when these moments come along, we can only try our best and hope it works out. What's your reaction time?

-Michael, 24, California.

First off, everyone wants our troops home, it is very dangerous over there in the Middle East, but we cannot leave until the job is done. Our troops are risking their lives everyday for the safety of their country, family, and friends. So don't yell at the president to bring them home, cause they signed up for it and knew what they were getting into. Iraq attacked us first, so we have the right to protect our country, and yes people will die, but that's life. When Japan attacked Pearl Harbor did we just say, [oh] well and sit back

and relax? No, we went to war, and [won]. We finished the job, and
then came home. That's what we need to do now. Thank you to
the troops for keeping me safe, and risking your lives for me, God
bless you!!!!

-Suzy Dotson, 15, California

After 9/11, people began to create conspiracy theories concerning who was really behind the attacks. Through work, I have recently met a man—let's call him Bob—who is one of the thirty
three million Americans who believe the theories that our government blew its own people up. Thirty three million is about eleven
percent of this country's population, and it worries me. It isn't impossible for the theory to be true, but for it to be true I think it has
to make sense. I want people to realize that the American government is more than able to attack our country because it is run by
humans—and worse yet, human politicians who want and need
power. Yet, I am still unconvinced that our government has indeed
bombed its own people.

Bob was kind enough to email me information on the theory,
and I was amazed at the passion these people had for convincing
people that it was true. Still, I've watched the videos on YouTube
and read some of the writings and have yet to be convinced. I realize that people bring into question President Bush's tie to oil in the
Middle East, his ties to the underground organization "Skull and
Bones," but I really want to know what the motivation would be
behind this kind of attack.

My concern isn't the "proof" that the conspiracy theorists have
presented. I'm concerned with the fact that thirty three million
people have such a lack of faith in our government. The theories
mention the involvement of not just one American president but
many. If the American citizens have such a lack of faith in our lead-

ership, how can the country be a safe haven for immigrants, the land of the free, or the America so many of us *need* for it to be?

This is America; this is the greatest country to live in. If twenty million illegal immigrants will come here from Mexico and other countries and withstand the low wages and forms of slavery some experience just to be here, then you have to see that we are the best. I know to some people that sounds vain, but tell me what other country you would rather live in? Iran? Iraq? How about France, where extreme Muslims have conducted violent marches? How about Spain, where Muslims quickly attacked their train station and killed their citizens because they could? As nice as Canada is, their government structure would never work here in America, because Americans are too independent. What I mean by that is we don't depend on our government for most things, and if you are one of those people who has never had a job and lives off of welfare, you need to get up and do something with your life.

Here in America, we are debating over national heath care because most of us realize the toll that would take on our country economically and physically. What I mean by physically is this: I have relatives who live in Canada, and when they have major surgeries they come to America because they perceive that their hospitals are not safe. By socializing heath care, you put yourself at risk. Doctors lose incentive to perform surgeries correctly. I hear that doctors do their jobs not only for money but to help people, and even though this is true, the money and freedom to run their businesses their ways sure as heck helps. The belief that people need their government to survive is false.

Our government isn't us as a nation, and yet we sit back and let them represent us to the rest of the world. Remember that the government is here for us, and if we the people let them pass laws, create regulations, and control us, then little by little we lose our God-given freedom. Any and all theories that pose our government leaders as evil dictators are to be dismissed because of the lack of proof and out of respect to the position in which these leaders take on.

Don't forget: We are one nation under God, indivisible, and with liberty and justice for all.

Chapter Three:

BREAKING AND ENTERING

*"Ours is an open and accepting society, and has historically provided
an avenue for lawful immigration to all those willing to accept the
responsibilities of citizenship."*
- Spencer Bachus

THE reality of immigration has been twisted and turned. My family is a good example of what immigration should be. My relatives immigrated to America legally and respected the fact that America didn't just let people in. They understood that to be a part of the great country of the United States, they had to work for it.

This is how I see it. I'll give you two scenarios.

First: Imagine you want to join this really great club, but to do it you have to sign up and be initiated. You don't care what you have to do, you just want in. You jump over lion pits, leap through fire hoops, you ignore everyone who tells you to take the easy route, and in the end you are welcomed into the greatest club in the world. You feel absolute pride at the fact that you did everything right and nothing wrong. Congratulations; you are now a part of the club.

Second: Let's say you decide to listen to those whispers in your ear and take a shortcut. You sneak past the initiation, and the next thing you know, you can't relax. You're constantly scanning the faces of the other club members, desperate that no one discover your secret. You feel as if everyone can see right through you, as if everyone around you is giving you dirty looks. And you can't enjoy the benefits that the others praise every day. This is your life because you didn't do it the right way, because you snuck into a club that now does not fully respect you. You feel alone and insignificant, and you don't get any congratulations; instead, the members work to get your ass kicked out of *their* club. They don't want a member in their club who can't respect the rules. If they let you in, then the integrity of the club depletes.

Another analogy: You wouldn't let people just come into your home and act like it's theirs, would you? No, of course not. But that's what happens every time an illegal immigrant comes into America. America is *my* home. I'm its security system, and if I become useless and don't protect what is mine, then catastrophe occurs. I've already seen crime rates increase because of illegal immigrants. I took multiple law enforcement classes that informed us that illegal immigrants were taking drastic moves to hide their identity, such as burning off their fingerprints or getting their fingerprints surgically changed.

Living in California, I've seen countless pictures of illegal immigrants hiding in trunks of cars or running across freeways in hopes of making it over before being hit by a car. I think my biggest pet peeve is the fact that we need signs on our freeways warning of families crossing. It's absolutely devastating to know that while you're going seventy miles per hour down the freeway, you could hit a mom clinging to her child. In the end, you would be tried for manslaughter and probably serve ten years in prison for killing an illegal immigrant because we have people in this country who refuse to fight for their own people. God forbid something like that should happen to you, but if it did, to whom will you turn for protection? It seems to me that illegal immigrants, from any country, have more rights and protection in America than the

Americans. The best example I can give you is the Ignacio Ramos and Jose Compean case. These two men are two border patrol agents who shot an illegal immigrant in the butt—an illegal immigrant who had been driving a van full of illegal drugs over the border into America. Ramos and Compean are now serving over ten year sentences.

I have a message for all of you who believed that this was justice.

For every time you are trapped in a burning building and praying for a fireman to come and rescue you, for every time you are being robbed and are hoping someone is calling the police to come save you, and for every time you decide to go clubbing over the border and have a run-in with muggers and your heart aches with hope that a border patrol agent might chance by and help you, I want you to remember Ignacio Ramos and Jose Compean.

Because of faulty evidence or lack thereof, the jury and judges have condemned two of our American citizens to a decade of jail time. They were doing a job that almost no one wants to do, protecting our borders, and when they did something right they got thrown in jail for it. Reports say agents Ignacio Ramos and Jose Compean withheld information concerning the incident. The facts have been smudged from the first day of this case. I hear people say the agents got what they deserve because "it's the law," but last time I checked it was illegal to come over the American border without a green card, work pass, or citizenship, not to mention with over seven hundred pounds of drugs in the vehicle.

What I'm wondering is why in the world Ramos and Compean are being prosecuted for breaking a law that was never intended to be used against law enforcement agents. If the men who are supposed to carry a gun and use it if necessary are in jail, what chance to any of us civilians have when we plead self defense?

Last time I checked, I lived in America. We are the Land of The

Free, the nation that *protects* its citizens, not condemns them. A majority of people expected our president to pardon these men and put this ridiculousness to an end, but they were disappointed.

So, for the judges and jury who put these two men in jail, I want you to remember that you will get yours. There are true American people who know that these two men did their jobs. It is absolutely the most absurd thing I have heard. I may be only nineteen, but you'd better believe that I won't let these things happen in my county, the land of the *free*, if I can help it. I will do what it takes to end this injustice.

In addition to my particular outrage for the Ramos and Compean case, it boggles my mind when illegal immigrants hold marches in our streets with signs bashing America and we just sit back and enjoy the show. See, I thought that *Americans* had the right to free speech in this country. Apparently I'm wrong, because I have yet to see mass arrests of illegal immigrants during these events. I feel like the people who are breaking so many rules in our county are right there in the streets and yet our police officers can't arrest them because it's free speech, or because the legal suits say its within the immigrants' civil rights. I understand that a good number of those protesters are citizens, but to me they are disgracing our country by taking the sides of people who are willing to use it without giving anything back. Illegal immigrants don't pay taxes and don't have insurance; have you ever been in a car accident when an illegal immigrant is at fault? I know plenty of people who get frustrated because they are left with the whole bill. There's a reason that it's illegal to drive without insurance, and there's a reason why you can't come here illegally.

Are you still with me? I know it seems harsh and coldhearted, but I believe that for a country to survive, rules have got to be followed. Maybe you agree, or maybe you're crushing the pages of this book in your hands. Either way, it's what I believe, and what

I believe is because of what I've seen, heard, and felt throughout my life.

I was listening to Rush Limbaugh, the god of AM radio, and heard him naming off all these immigration rules. He calls them the Limbaugh Laws, and I'd like to share with you that transcript from the show.

START TRANSCRIPT

"All right, immigration proposals under discussion. Let me add mine to the mix. I want to call this proposal the Limbaugh Laws. Here they are. First, if you immigrate to the United States of America, you must speak the native language. You have to be a professional or an investor. We are not going to take unskilled workers. You will not be allowed. There will be no special bilingual programs in the schools, no special ballots for elections; no government business will be conducted in your native language. Foreigners will not have the right to vote, I don't care how long they are here, nor will they ever be allowed to hold political office. According to the Limbaugh Laws, if you're in our country, you cannot be a burden to taxpayers.

You are not entitled, ever, to welfare, to food stamps, or other government goodies. You can come if you invest here, but it must be an amount equal to 40,000 times the daily minimum wage. If you don't now have that amount of money, you can't come and invest. You have to stay home. If you do come and you want to buy land, okay, but we're going to restrict your options. You will not be allowed to buy waterfront property in the United States. That will be reserved for citizens naturally born in this country.

In fact, as a foreigner, you must relinquish individual rights to property.

These are the Limbaugh Laws. Another thing. You don't have the right to protest when you come here. You're allowed no demonstrations, you cannot wave a foreign flag, no political organizing, no bad-mouthing our president or his policies, or you get sent home. You're a foreigner. You shut your mouth or you get out, and if you come here illegally, you go straight to jail and we're going to hunt you down 'til we find you.

I can imagine many of you think that the Limbaugh Laws are pretty harsh. I imagine today some of you probably are going, "Yeah! Yeah!" Well, let me tell you this, folks. Every one of the laws I just mentioned are actual laws of Mexico, today. I just read you Mexican immigration law. That's how the Mexican government handles immigrants to their country. Yet Mexicans and others come here illegally, they protest in our streets, they get on our welfare program, and we have members of the United States Senate, both parties, doing handstands and back flips, going through every contortion possible to allow it to continue so that it doesn't make these people mad, resulting in votes against these linguini-spined populations.

This is more than a double standard. It is an indication of just how gutless people in charge in this country are to protect the identity of this country. They don't care about border security, I know the ports deal notwithstanding, they're not doing a thing to shore up the border, because that might make somebody mad. It's a good thing there

are a whole lot of Arab voters in this country or the port
deal would have gone through, too."

END TRANSCRIPT

How did we get to this point? I've been paying pretty close attention to the economy lately, as I'm sure most of you have been,
and I wonder if people realize how greatly illegal immigrants affect
the economy.

Here's what I got: Illegal immigrants don't pay taxes. One of
my teachers tried to convince me that illegal immigrants actually
do pay taxes because they want to feel like a part of our society.
That's a load of bull. I want to know how many *American* citizens
would still pay taxes if they didn't have to.

Next: Bank of America was recently involved in a scandal of
creating bank accounts and other incentives for illegal immigrants
without asking for background information. No
w, Bank of America is buying out some of these banks that are
closing down. Bank of America is growing. These current banks
and private businesses that are closing down, and which the government is bailing out, gave loans to people who couldn't even
speak English. They gave loans to those people who couldn't even
afford it, and the banks knew that. They knew they were dealing
with customers that didn't have what it took to buy a home, and
now the responsible taxpayer has to pay for it. Meanwhile people
like my parents—who had ten kids and moved twelve times, always to a bigger and better home—sucked up the years of renting
and living in small homes because they weren't ready to buy. They
waited until they had the money to invest properly.

The illegal immigrants, who aren't paying taxes but are working for corporations, or for your next-door neighbor cutting grass,
are earning our American dollar and not contributing to our so-

ciety. They are getting free passes, but remember: Nothing is free. Someone still has to pay for those immigrants' free rides and that someone will be the American citizen.

Remember: Everything we do in life has a domino affect, and this is just the beginning.

Chapter Four

SEX AND ICE CREAM

"Maturity begins to grow when you can sense your concern for others outweighing your concern for yourself."
- John MacNoughton

For young adults, sex has got to be one of the most confusing, scary, and appealing things in the world. Every parent should strive to explain what sex really is to his or her children. Here's how I see it and try to explain it to my peers:

Sex is, in no way, shape, or form, a bad thing. But there is certainly a wrong time, a wrong place, and the wrong person with whom to explore that natural curiosity. Children and young adults have to understand that sex is something that should never be explored on impulse. The way I see it, sex is sort of like ice cream. You shouldn't have ice cream before dinner, but some of us do and end up getting a stomachache. Of course, just because you had ice cream before dinner doesn't mean you can never have ice cream again or that you get kicked out of the dinner club. When people make mistakes, they should learn from them but try to make as few of them as possible. But I digress; if you wait and have ice cream after dinner, more than likely, no stomachache will follow.

One of the many books on sex that I have read and that has impacted me is Dr. Laura Schlessinger's *The Proper Care and Feeding of Marriage*. The book is absolutely wonderful and applicable to any and all types of marriage and relationships, and has taught me a great deal. But I'm not here to sell it. I'm here to tell you what I've learned. I've learned that marriage, sex, children, death, and life are all connected. Therefore, we must be very cautious with what we decide to do.

I, for one, do not like to think that sex is just for making babies, because it's not. Sex, making love, getting down and dirty—whatever you choose to call it—is a way for two people to connect on levels beyond even the deepest friendship. Doesn't that just sound wonderful? But it isn't as easy as picking someone that makes you feel warm and then going for it. Everything we do has consequences, good and bad.

I think it's sometimes easy for parents and youth to think that sex has few consequences as long as one goes about it the right way. We often hear about "safe sex" and think that if we follow "safe sex" methods everything will be okay. I can't stress how backwards this is. Safe sex is anything but safe. The government wants us to use contraception at a young age to prevent pregnancy. Well, I've got an idea that's a little farfetched: What if kids just didn't have sex? I know what you're thinking— "In *this* society? But how?"

I believe that parents need to teach their kids to have integrity.

I knew a girl who wasn't having sex during high school, but her mother refused to believe her. So her mother took her to the doctor, requested birth control, and made her daughter take it. The daughter was angry, sad, and felt a little cheap. Her mother wouldn't listen to her when she insisted she wasn't having sex. Almost a year later, the girl looked at her boyfriend and thought, *I'm already on birth control, what's the point of not fooling around?* In other words, she felt like the battle she was fighting, abstinence, was useless. I will never forget this girl, and I will never forget her mother. There are thousands of mothers just like this girl's, who believe that their daughters are going to have sex anyway so they just hand over the birth control, satisfied with their "parental duty." I feel that if that mother had had faith in her daughter and treated her with respect, then her daughter wouldn't have given in to something she had been fighting so hard against.

Now, after sex, there is always the chance that babies will come into the picture. Babies are not dirty little things. Babies are a part of their parents, and there is no reason why a baby should not be loved. If you feel that you can't take proper care of your child, there are parents all over the world who would love to adopt. I can only imagine how hard it would be to give my baby to another couple, but I think it would be even harder to live with myself after an abortion. Knowing that I killed the life that was so a part of me before it could decide what it wanted for itself would be brutal.

I'm sorry if you, reader, have taken the road that has left so many women and men feeling depressed and alone. You are *not* alone and never will be. Even if you took that road and regret that decision, there are ways to amend that loss. My mother had ten kids and seven miscarriages. I cried with real tears for each of those miscarriages. I cried because I knew that I just lost a little brother or sister and that they would never know the joy of life like I have. I cried because women can seem so eager to throw away a life that *they* created and just weren't tough enough to handle. I fully understand that some women are put into situations that they can't control. I understand that rape happens and many women can't handle having the babies of their rapists. But I urge women to realize that two wrongs do not make a right. That just because they were hurt does not make it right to hurt the child. I want women to understand that something bigger has happened. That being pregnant is a blessing, never a curse.

Something to think about is this: Let's say you have a child and let him or her grow up. You would never imagine killing your son or daughter, would you? Yet, we have women who are more than willing to kill off the babies in their wombs. I've heard the argument countless times that a woman can't give up a child for adoption because she grows attached to it. It's better, they say, for her to kill it now. I have never heard a more selfish thing in my life. Some women out there think, *It's my baby, and if I can't have it, neither can anyone else,* and then kill their babies. It makes me want to vomit.

A lot of people believe that abortion is a woman's choice because it only affects her. I'm here to tell you that that is the biggest lie ever told. If a woman gets pregnant, that means there's a father, and that means there are two sets of grandparents. There are nieces and nephews. There are aunts and uncles, future godmothers and godfathers. There is a whole world out there that is awaiting the person who will bring it the cure for cancer, or the person who will truly inspire and attain peace. Will you be responsible for killing humanity's hopes and dreams?

A majority of America criticizes China for killing off any baby that isn't a boy. Yet we sit here and justify our own slaughtering of America's future generations. In that way, we are the same as China, the same as Africa and the Muslim countries that devalue life.

Safe sex is nonexistent, and abortion is just another way to run.

Another subject that ties into all of this is pornography. When I think porn I think of men, but in reality there are women who watch and, of course, participate in porn as well. I wrote an Internet article concerning porn and would like to share it with you.

> Adult porn is women and men willing to sell their bodies visually for money. Pornography is, in my opinion, a visual form of prostitution. You might think that's radical, but stay with me here and I'll tell you why I think that.

If you think about it as a job, prostitution—women making a good amount of money to have sex with men at their own free will—doesn't seem that bad. But what has made the act of prostitution illegal? The string of lies, violence, drugs, abuse, and death that tie into the world of prostitution is remarkable. You can't just see a subject as one issue, because every one issue is made up of multiple things that make it whole.

Some classify prostitution as an art, but they are just making an excuse to allow it. I personally like some nude art and still think art is what it is. But any person who claims that porn is an art is blind; that's like saying rape is making love. They consist of similar, if not the same, elements but are two completely different things.

I don't see how a man or a woman can be liberated if they send the message out that they're cheap and don't hold their bodies sacred. I read an article written by a woman who believed that because rape occurred before porn was created it didn't attribute to the urge to commit the rape. Let me clarify this by saying the Egyptian kings would watch women dance, would lust after them and take many to their beds. People have to understand that porn as been around since the beginning of time, not through the Internet or magazines or even books, but through dances and prostitution. Porn comes in all shapes and sizes, and it steals away what sex should be and what love could be.

To say that porn is an expression of art or can help you with your sex life is invalid. There are plenty of men and women who are have waited to have sex until marriage and are going on twenty great years. There are others who had sex before marriage, without the porn, and are going on fifteen. But I guarantee you that the woman who married the man who had porn magazines under the mattress and in the car is always going to worry, and will always wonder, *Is he cheating on me? Is he thinking of that woman on page 26 of* Playboy *magazine while we have sex?*

Think about it.

Let me say right now that I don't share well, even when it comes to the imaginary women on page twenty six of *Playboy* magazine. I don't think porn is good for the minds of teenage or college guys, and I'm sad to say that women are starting to act like such "players" that I can't see the difference between the sexes. There are so many romantic comedies out there that always seem to have main characters that sleep around as if that's normal. There was one movie that I didn't practically like because the main character really got under my skin. The movie is called *Because I Said So*, staring Mandy Moore and Diane Keaton.

The movie is about a mother's (Diane Keaton) need to find a boyfriend for her daughter (Mandy Moore). During the film, Diane Keaton finds a perfect man for Mandy Moore and the two young people end up going out. At the same time, Mandy Moore meets another perfect guy who has a son and great hair, not to mention plays guitar. During the movie, Mandy Moore is dating both of men, each of whom is unaware of the other. Of course, Mandy Moore ends up sleeping with both of them and the movie spirals down from there.

It bugged me so much that women are continually being portrayed as sex fiends who play the control game with men because they can. It annoys the hell out of me to know that girls are seeing this and not thinking how wrong it was of Mandy Moore to sleep with two men at the same time but instead wondering who she'd end up with. It annoyed me when Mandy Moore was chatting with her two sisters, and when they found out she was doing both men, they giggled like it was something to be proud of. I think the best movie that portrayed the consequences of having sex outside of marriage was *Juno*. That movie was fantastic because it showed that even a teenager could see that she wasn't ready for something so beyond her years. Even though she had sex thinking only of herself, her pregnancy taught her that her baby was more important than herself. The movie is great, and I don't want to give away the ending because I think everyone should see it.

Wow, now I feel like Roger Ebert, and you're getting two thumbs up for *Juno*!

From the Youth:

"Abortion: One day people will look back and say "this was the time when the culture thought it was, 'OK to kill its kids before they were born.' Birth Control: People want to turn sex into a form of entertainment, when the only reason it exists is for reproduction. High School: Being social, by itself, doesn't make you a better person. It teaches you how to be more likable, how to manipulate others, and how to manipulate yourself. It is a search for the easy way, clouded by sentiment and stunted by impatience. Culture: 1. To misunderstand is to breed misunderstanding. 2. Will you think for your emotions or will you let emotions think for you?"

-Adam Black, 21, California

"When I was just 21 I found out I was pregnant. I was living in Kansas City at the time, had little family and few friends. The

35

dad of course took off. I was working at a department store and was living in an apartment with a roommate. I was devastated and had thoughts of keeping it, adoption, and even abortion. I was actually at work one day and was fumbling through the phone book looking for abortion clinics and somehow stumbled across a Christian based crisis pregnancy center instead. I gave them a call and made an appointment. I went in and spoke with them, they prayed for me, let me know I wasn't alone and really encouraged me. They were wonderful women and I left there feeling positive and excited about having a baby. However, I still felt ashamed for being a young unwed mom.

A few months went by and I finally told my family up in Michigan. Their reactions were far better than what I expected. They were actually excited. I was about 6 months pregnant and had my first real doctor's appointment. My roommate Jenna came with me. At that appointment I found out I was having a girl and also found out something that was going to drastically change my life and my new daughter's life. The doctor and the woman that did the ultrasound came into the room and stated they had seen a shadow on the baby's back that they were somewhat concerned about. They reassured me it was probably nothing more than just a pesky shadow but handed me a referral paper and sent me on my way to the hospital across the street for a more detailed ultrasound.

After that ultrasound I was called into an office of a doctor and I remember all he said was: "Do you know what Spina Bifida is?" I looked at him with a blank look because I had no idea. He then explained that's what my baby had. The shadow was actually a sack due to a hole in her back down by the tailbone, and the sack held her nerves to her spine that were actually protruding from this hole, and it's possible she could be in a wheelchair and [he] explained all the problems associated with Spina Bifida. I was in shock. I immediately called my family and headed on into work.

I told my boss what was going on and word quickly spread to all the employees throughout the store. I was immediately put on prayer chains from Arizona to South Africa. The people I worked with started approaching me telling me they [were] praying for us and more specifically for the use of [my daughter's] legs. What really touched me was when customers, complete strangers, would approach me and tell me they were praying for me and my baby. It really touched me. Even after she was born I still had customers coming up to me asking me how my baby was and as they walked away they always ended 'I have been praying for you guys.'

It just blew me away that these complete strangers had so much compassion for me and my baby.

The doctors never gave me answers on how well my baby would do because they just didn't know. Each case involving Spina Bifida is so drastically different [that] it's hard to tell until after the baby is born. One thing doctors told me was one way we would know if she might be able to walk is if she comes out kicking her legs. I remember being on the surgery table because I had to get a C-section and my roommate being in the surgical room with me. I remember her yelling, "She's kicking, Renee!"

I knew right then I had a miracle baby who was a fighter. I named her Hope. They immediately rushed her to the local children's hospital to repair her back. She was there for the first month of her life. Being a young mother with a child that has Spina Bifida has had its ups and downs but I really feel if it weren't for all of the prayers we wouldn't be so lucky. Hope is now 3 years old and walks and talks like a normal child. She beat the odds and never had to have the aid of braces, walkers, or a wheel chair. At 8 months old she had to get a shunt for her hydrocephalus but we have been blessed to have no problems with the shunt so far. She does have some problems with her bowels and we have to catheterize her 5 times a day.

I have been to the Myelo clinics at children's hospitals, and I have seen all the kids in wheelchairs and I just can't help but to thank God for his miracle. Hope and I are very happy and we are surrounded by people who just love her. She is an absolute joy in my life and I wouldn't trade her for the world."

-Renee, 25, Michigan

I'd like to end this chapter with this forward that someone posted in a bulletin on MySpace.

The Four Boyfriends

Once upon a time there was a Princess who had four
boyfriends.
She loved the fourth boyfriend the most and adorned him
with rich robes and treated him to the finest of delicacies. She
gave him nothing but the best.
She also loved the third boyfriend very much and was always
showing him off to neighboring kingdoms. However, she
feared that one day he would leave her for another.
She also loved her second boyfriend. He was her confidante
and was always kind, considerate and patient with her.
Whenever this girl faced a problem, she could confide in him,
and he would help her get through the difficult times.
The girl's first boyfriend was a very loyal partner and had
made great contributions in maintaining her wealth and
kingdom.
However, she did not love the first boyfriend although he
loved her deeply; she hardly took notice of him!

One day, the girl fell ill and she knew her time was short. She thought of her luxurious life and wondered, "I now have four boyfriends with me, but when I die, will I be alone."

Thus, she asked the fourth boyfriend, "I loved you the most, endowed you with the finest clothing and showered great care over you. Now that I'm dying, will you follow me and keep me company?"

"No way!" replied the fourth boyfriend and he walked away without another word.

His answer cut like a sharp knife right into her heart.

The sad girl then asked the third boyfriend, "I loved you all my life. Now that I'm dying, will you follow me and keep me company?"

"No!" replied the third boyfriend. "Life is too good! When you die, I'm going to marry someone else!"

Her heart sank and turned cold. She then asked the second boyfriend, "I have always turned to you for help and you've always been there for me. When I die, will you follow me and keep me company?"

"I'm sorry, I can't help you out this time," replied the second boyfriend. "At the very most, I can only walk with you to your grave."

His answer struck her like a bolt of lightning, and the girl was devastated.

Then a voice called out: "I'll go with you. I'll follow you no matter where you go."

The girl looked up, and there was her first boyfriend. He was very skinny as he suffered from malnutrition and neglect.

Greatly grieved, the girl said, "I should have taken much better care of you when I had the chance!"

In truth, you have four boyfriends in your lives:

Your fourth boyfriend is your body. No matter how much

time and effort you lavish in making it look good, it will leave
you when you die.
Your third boyfriend is your possessions, status and wealth.
When you die, it will all go to others.
Your second boyfriend is your family and friends. No matter
how much they have been there for you, the furthest they can
stay by you is up to the grave.
And your first boyfriend is your spirit. Often neglected in
pursuit of wealth, power and pleasures of the world.
However, your spirit is the only thing that will follow you
wherever you go. Cultivate, strengthen and cherish it now, for
it is the only part of you that will follow you to the throne of
God and continue with you throughout eternity.
Thought for the day: Remember, when the world pushes you
to your knees, you're in the perfect position to pray.
Being happy doesn't mean everything's perfect.
It means you've decided to see beyond the imperfections.

Chapter Five

CIVIL CRUTCHES

"I have never let my schooling interfere with my education."
- Mark Twain

I THINK that government officials claim to give the youth rights, but what they are taking away is parents' rights. There are times when the government has no business getting involved in a child's life and others when it's important they create boundaries. Let me explain with an analogy: Parents who say "yes" to their kids more than they say "no" are more likely to have children who end up in jail, get involved in illegal activities, or start having pre-marital sex. If parents don't set boundaries for their children, the children get confused. Children aren't meant to have too much power, because they are not mentally or physically ready for it. However, there have been multiple schools that have taken it upon themselves to play parent.

Middle schools are now passing out contraceptives to their students, a phenomenon that isn't new, but of which people seem to be unaware. Kids under the age of eighteen are considered minors; therefore, the people who make decisions for them are supposed to be their parents. Yet, the schools seem to think that *they* are the parents. I know plenty of parents who do not want their kids having sex and getting free contraceptives without their knowledge. The problem is that the government isn't listening. It seems to think that neglectful parents don't need to know what their children are doing. What if a parent isn't neglectful and just told his or her child "no," but the child told the school or government official differently?

I'll give you a scenario: There's a rebelling teen that wants to be sexually active, even though her parents have forbidden it. The girl goes to school and tells a sob story that convinces the school to hand her a contraceptive without contacting her parents. It sounds like something that couldn't happen, but it has.

In October 2007, Lis Wiehl of Fox News wrote wrote an online article called "Birth Control at Middle School?" The article addresses and analyzes the implications of a school in Maine that actually agreed to pass out birth control to kids as young as eleven. Here is an excerpt from the article:

> Middle school students are at the center of a controversial movement, as the Portland School Board recently gave the green light to their medical staff to prescribe children — as young as 11 years old — prescription birth control medications. Meanwhile, the tweens don't have to notify their parents. Is this insane? Yes — and maybe even illegal!

> Here's the background: the proposal, from the Portland Division of Public Health, calls for the independently operated health care center at King Middle School to provide a variety of services to students — including immunizations and physical checkups AND birth control medications and counseling for sexually transmitted diseases.

> The plan, offered by city health officials, makes King Middle School the first junior high in Maine to make a full range of contraception available to students in grades

six through eight ... repeat, sixth through eighth grade! Health care professionals advised the school committee that the proposal was necessary in order for the clinic to serve students who were engaging in risky behavior.

By providing children with contraceptives, the government and schools send the message to kids that they can involve themselves in adult activities and get bailed out—even without their parents' knowledge. The problem, in this case, is that children are burdened with what may have initially seemed like a good time but instead turns out to be a living hell. It's like they wear chains on their shoulders that would never have been there if they were allowed to live life as kids should. We have people in power right now making laws that will affect *us*, the youth, and not them. By the time the laws start to show their real colors, the people who initiated them will be dead. It will be us who will suffer or benefit. Furthermore, I believe that the occurrences of teen pregnancy, AIDS, and teen suicide would all go down if we stopped giving children adult responsibilities.

I was home-schooled until I reached my second year of high school, and then I attended a public school. It was my choice and one I don't regret, though I wasn't a typical teenager. I like to think of myself as a strong person, and though I was weaker then than I am now, I still believe I was stronger than some of my peers. I was stronger in the sense that I never gave in, and I questioned everything to make sure I understood and could eventually make my own choices. I always challenged my teachers and watched as my peers just accepted things and didn't question, even if they secretly wanted to. I really didn't learn much academically speaking, to tell you the truth. I was busy acting in plays and sleeping in class, eating in class, and making enemies. I graduated early to get away from the people and so-called "education." I'm better for it, and I'm here writing this book now.

I think there is an amazing amount of wise youth out there; they just need to speak up loudly enough for the rest to hear.

Of course, there are many things besides sex affecting the youth. Illegal drugs have been all the rage for years, and though I never witnessed kids smoking marijuana in front of me, I always knew who was doing it. My peers who did smoke didn't actually keep it a secret, but they didn't flaunt it, either. I've taken law enforcement classes and discussed that other countries that have legalized drugs boast lower crime rates. The reason their crime rates are lower, however, is because the drugs are legal and, therefore, participating in them isn't counted as a crime. This differs from the U.S., where drugs like marijuana, cocaine, and heroin are illegal, and whose usage does get counted as a crime. Regardless of legality, drugs are still harmful and disgusting.

I've talked with high-schoolers and college students about many issues, some consisting of drinking laws, driving laws, academic practices, and their thoughts on them. One of the complaints I hear the most from high-schoolers is about the required classes they take in school. Some believe that certain subjects should not be required to graduate or be accepted into college. This subject, however, is trivial to the bigger issues affecting younger generations.

A larger issue that I think affects a number of the youth is alcohol consumption. I've talked with plenty of people under twenty-one who like to drink for many reasons, be it for partying or just relaxation. I, too, have wondered if we should fight to lower the alcohol consumption age, but I figure that it really wouldn't benefit our society; the last thing we need is for the teens that want to abuse alcohol to have easier access to it. Still, it amazes me that at eighteen, I can legally purchase (and participate) in porn, vote for

the future president, smoke cigarettes, pierce my body with millions of holes, party all night, buy my own car, and *own a gun*, but
I can't drink a glass of wine with dinner. Now, the things I've just
listed are things that can only be done by legal adults, but these
activities are still practiced by young teenagers.

Now, the news is reporting that college students are trying to
lower the drinking age, and people are actually paying attention.
One of the reasons they want to lower laws is to prevent underage drinking. That made a warning bell in my head go off, because
lowering the legal alcohol consumption age isn't going to prevent
anything; if anything, underage drinking is going to get worse,
thanks to eighteen-year-old kids buying alcohol for their younger
siblings or friends. It doesn't take a genius to figure that out. Trust
me, I wish I could order a beer with my dinner, but I'm not going
to fight to lower the legal age, because in the end it's going to do
the youth more harm than good.

I received an email from a high school student named Joseph.
As I read his email and he discussed the education system, a light
bulb went off in my mind. I want to share with you his email before I go on:

"My views on education: This is one of my biggest pas-
sions. This is where change occurs. If we have any hope
of bettering our nation, economy, or life, it needs to have
a strong basis. This basis begins with a great education.
The best way to make a difference is to begin with the next
generation.

My views on the teachers of today: It turns out that
there is really a difference [between] a teacher and a babysitter. A teacher is someone who cares, listens, and wants
[his or her] students to succeed. A babysitter just watches
and tells what to do. I really think I go to a school where

just babysitters are hired and told to look after thirty kids and make sure everyone stays safe. They are just there for the paycheck. They do nothing to ensure things are being learned. They read from a book that has the answers given and then when they get stuck, they ask me for help. Does that sound right? Is a student supposed to being teaching the class? I mean, I don't have a degree or a paycheck. It is sad when our own public school systems set their students up for failure. Maybe I should have stayed in private school"?

-Joseph Huckabee, 17, California

When I finished reading that, I realized what high school really was for me: a daycare. I think the only teachers that taught me anything were my English teachers, one history teacher, and one fashion teacher. I remember there were some classes where I didn't do anything, where we wasted the period just "hanging out." At first this was great and then later through the year most of us didn't even want to go to those classes anymore. There were students who came for roll call and left soon after. I wonder what our tax dollars are going to and what our hard-earned cash is paying the teachers to teach us. There's a movie called *Charlie Bartlett*, an amusing film about high school life revolving around a boy who isn't always liked, and whose goal throughout the film is to be popular. At one point, his mother asks why he has to worry about being popular. In response, he said, "Is there anything more important?" She thinks about it and then shakes her head, saying, "Nothing comes to mind."

It is, for the most part, true. I'm not saying that the school I went to was awful or that I learned nothing, because I learned a lot of things. However, the things I learned weren't academic lessons so much as life lessons. It was when the schools started telling me what to eat that I began to get angry. Laws passed in California recently stopped the selling of candy bars and chips that weren't "baked." The baked chips ended up being pretty good, but the loss of candy bars meant we couldn't sell candy to raise money for clubs and school activities.

I remember many times when birthdays came up and students would bring cake to school for lunch to share with friends, but after the laws were passed, this was no longer allowed. Or when my neighbor, who was a part of the cheerleading squad, wanted to pass out cupcakes to her team and was rejected. Administrators claimed it was to help kids eat less junk food at school because the obesity rate was up in California. My problem with this was the fact that high school students are only at school a certain amount of hours. Once they go home, they are going to eat whatever they want.

Another recent change: Cell phones are no longer allowed at schools in my area. This sounds good because, logically, students shouldn't have cell phones at school. However, I have a dilemma with this. While students shouldn't use cell phones during class, it's important that they have them during lunch, at break or in an emergency. I'm sorry to say that, in this tech savvy world, parents have only that way to contact students, and students need phones to contact each other during lunch. Trust me, it is not easy finding your friend in a mass of students during lunch, and sitting alone for a half an hour is not amusing. Yes, there are ways for a parent to contact a student during school, but there aren't afterwards. Cell phones have their place in school, and it's not fair to punish the students who use them responsibly because some students abuse them.

There was another regulation the school snuck into the rule-book. When I was in high school, parents and graduated students

47

could walk around campus during the day and visit teachers' classrooms, keeping in mind that they needed to respect the teachers' decisions if they were asked to leave. This rule was changed. When I went to visit my old high school, which three of my siblings currently attend, I was told that I couldn't enter the campus. The women at the front desk told my mom to wait in certain areas but not to walk around. There was one time when I went with my brother to help him pull out of the main high school and transfer to another one and they wouldn't let me on campus. I was told to leave and that he would call me on their school phone. Later, when I approached the school about certain legislation being passed that would directly affect our youth, I was pushed away. The ladies at the front desk didn't want to hear that someone had a complaint (though it wasn't so much a complaint as concern). The indoctrination of our children in schools is going to go unnoticed unless parents keep up with the system.

There is an unbalanced rulebook by which schools are playing by, and it's affecting our kids. I realize this is just my school district, but how many others are taking rights away from parents without anyone doing anything about it? The schools are using good ideas and intriguing words to meet their agendas. It doesn't sound so bad because people think the rules only apply when kids are in school. Kids are in school eight hours a day, five days a week—that adds up to forty hours a week that kids have to live under those absurd double standards. Forty hours a week where parents have no clue what they are teaching their kids. Forty hours where God isn't allowed because faith might offend the atheist. The public school system is a slow indoctrination of American children. What an odd world we live in where parents and teenagers sit back and let short chains be placed on their legs.

Chapter Six

MEDIA TRICKSTERS

*"Hollywood is a place where they'll pay you a thousand dollars for a kiss
and fifty cents for your soul."*
- Marilyn Monroe

I F I had the choice between watching television and reading a
book, I'd choose a book. Some people I know would rather play
video games, log onto MySpace, watch videos on YouTube, or read
People Magazine. But I have a question for all those who keep up
with the current Hollywood drama and music industry fiascos:
How much do the songs you listen to and movies you watch hin-
der your views on life? How much influence do your entertainment business idols have on you?

Some might shrug and argue that what they watch or listen to
doesn't affect them. Well, I beg to differ. When I do watch television, I watch the news, which sure as heck makes me doublethink
a lot. Watching the news makes me explode with emotions I didn't
even know existed inside of me. I yell more at my television when
I watch news than do many who watch football games. I laugh, I
get angry, and sometimes I cry. Sometimes it's because of the news
itself, but other times it's because I feel like the newscasters are
giving me their opinions instead of reporting the facts, and to me,
that's false reporting.

Maybe some of you are nodding your heads and remembering

the movie or famous person that affected you in a similar way. But there are so many hidden—and not so hidden—messages in films, and songs with prejudicial, sexist, and racist meanings that I just wonder why anyone would want to watch or listen to things so degrading to the human race. While I love how some rap and R&B songs have such great beats that my body automatically begins to dance, the problem with most of them is that they have lyrics I can't stand. And if I can't stand the lyrics, I won't listen to it, even if the beat is great.

The same thing goes for movies. Interestingly, though, the movies that bust the box office out of this world are almost always movies that are more conservative, patriotic, or funny but not crude. It's amazing that movies like *The Lion King* will be remembered for years and that movies like *Braveheart* motivate people to stand for what is theirs. It thrills me that movies like *I Am Legend* make more of an impact than controversial and highly publicized ones like *The Da Vinci Code*. It makes me laugh that *The Chronicles of Narnia* made more money then *The Golden Compass* could ever wish to make—when the latter's creator, Philip Pullman, believes that C.S. Lewis can't write and that *Narnia* was nothing compared to his film; and there are many others who think the same way. I believe that the American people have told the media over and over again what kinds of movies they want, and yet the industry still creates countless dull romances, comedies, dramas, and action movies that people don't even remember.

I watch TV Land with my family and enjoy its television shows like *I Love Lucy, The Andy Griffith Show*, and *Leave it to Beaver*. All of these shows normally have life lessons relayed throughout the story. That is largely missing from today's shows. A lot of cartoons have cute little lessons for younger children, but for teenagers, there are shows about drinkers, strippers, bad parents, and prejudice. I realize that a large number of young adults can relate to these shows, but I happen to be one who can't. I try watching MTV shows or The N shows, but it's hard to sit through the whole half hour. I feel like the shows never make me feel good after. They don't teach me anything, and they certainly don't make me want to emulate anyone on the screen.

I graduated early from high school just to get away from all the teenagers and so that I could move on. I couldn't relate to many of my peers, and it's hard spending eight hours a day surrounded by hundreds of people with whom you can't connect. I always joke that I was born thirty years old, but it's hard to back that up when I'm such a kid at heart. I just want to meet kids my age who aren't too busy wondering what Britney Spears is going to do next. It seems impossible to meet kids who have true respect for others; rather, when I say something, others my age call me "uptight." How can America continue to grow if its future generations don't care for and respect each other and the country in which they live?

All I have to say about the media is this: It's more fiction than fact.

I also have to say that I'm so sick of Hollywood destroying the youth. I barely even research the bands I listen to, let alone the stars of Hollywood. I'm not saying someone is unintelligent if he or she is a Hollywood junkie, but I'll amend a famous adage to say: You are what you read.

With that said, I admit it was amusing to me to hear what new mess Britney Spear's had walked into and I secretly rooting for her to do what everyone else knew she wouldn't and that was sober up. But now I'm sick of hearing about Britney Spears and her problems. She was pretty much my last hope that entertainment might stay human, but she fell. And I don't want to hear that another young actor, actress, or singer has died from an overdose or drinking and driving. Heath Ledger is still one of my favorite actors, and I refuse to accept the fact that the authorities no longer wish to research his death. I want answers. I want to know exactly why the young and the famous are so quickly destroyed.

2008 has been the year of Miley Cyrus and, to her credit, she really can sing, and her show on Disney is actually funny and entertaining. My problem with her and her *Vanity Fair* photo scandal (in which she was photographed wearing nothing but a sheet) isn't actually a problem with her, but with her parents. Even if Miley wanted to pose for those pictures, her *father* should have stood his ground and said no. That goes for Britney Spears's mom, who I don't believe truly cares for the wellbeing of her two daughters. That Jamie Lynn Spears had a baby at sixteen is old news. Now everyone is trying to get Miley in a hole, which she might end up leaping into unless her parents actually start acting like adults. It bothers me that the parents and adults in the entertainment business are so greedy and selfish that the wellbeing of their kids doesn't matter. Just for the record, I'm not placing Heath Ledger's family in this category; I actually think they cared. I believe their love for their son showed when they only let in about ten people for Heath's funeral, not to mention that they had it in Australia.

Until I see parents becoming responsible for what their kids watch, where they go and what they participate in, I will continue to be doubtful on the survival of future generations.

Chapter Seven

SALT AND PEPPER

"Racism is man's gravest threat to man - the maximum of hatred for a minimum of reason."
- Abraham J. Heschel

T HE amount of racism that still exists in this great country of the United States of America never ceases to amaze. Every time I hear people use the "n" word or terms like "cracker," my stomach turns and I just want to vomit. Yes, it's that bad. Yes, it does bother and offend people, and yes, it needs to stop.

I have to say—it's hard for me to comprehend the logic of racism. It's like people who make fun of someone for looking a certain way. It's not as if we sat there in our mothers' wombs and picked out our features or race. We have no control over what world we are born into or how we look to that world. What we do have power over is promotion, changing policy, taking a stand, and making a difference in the thought processes of the people around us.

When it comes to promoting political candidates or supporting movies or actors, we have to be careful not to support the wrong people. Here's what I mean: When choosing a presidential candidate, it's important to check out his or her voting record and history concerning the issues that matter to you. You aren't going to choose a candidate that associates with known racist groups or bigots. What about the music you listen to? I should hope that the music you listen to does not support something as disgusting and degrading as racism.

I realize and recognize that racism exists among many races, but I want to talk about the controversy on blacks and whites in America. I'm sorry to say that that type of racism is what I see and hear most often, though I'm not in any way ignoring anyone else who faces racism in his or her life; you have my prayers and support.

In any case, I never have understood the logic of rap artists who are African-American and use the "n" word. I never understood the logic that certain black people believe that it's *their* word because they're black. Because I was confused on this logic, I went to my local *Barnes and Noble* and purchased a book called *Stupid Black Men*, written by Larry Elder, a black radio host out of Los Angeles, California.

In the book, he talks about the consequences for blacks when they use the "n" word, using NBA Portland Trail Blazers player Darius Miles as an example. Elder reported that Miles "…defiantly shouted at his black coach, Maurice Cheeks, reportedly calling him 'N-ger,' during a team film session." Miles was later suspended for two days. He also made a statement apologizing for using the word.

Now, here's my question: Why do people believe that every problem can be fixed with an apology? There is no doubt that the constant sucking up to interest groups has demolished consequences to ill-informed actions in this country. So there is no such thing as a consequence for blacks when it comes to using the "n" word because they always argue that "my granddaddy was a slave of whites and someone owes me for that."

We can argue this point for hours or days, but the truth of the matter is that there is a loud and clear prejudice in this country from both sides of the "Oreo cookie," as I'll call it.

Here's an analogy on race using an Oreo cookie: On the outside we have a yummy, flavor-filled chocolate crust that tends to be too dry by itself. The cream that sits in the middle of the cookie is loved for its rich taste but tends to be too sweet without something to balance it out. So without the crust, the cream is to rich and without the cream, the crust is too dry—they need each other to be successful.

I realize I can't sum up the troubles of racism with a cookie, but I urge people to see it like a partnership or creating and keeping balance. We need to stop the division in this country. This country will never be truly the *United* States until we as a people understand and respect our differences and learn to thrive because of them.

I never want people to forget the horrid truth that whites did a great injustice to black Americans, but people cannot forget that some of the blacks today have twisted the wrists of the law and used it to excuse the problems in their lives. According to the National Center for Education Statistics concerning gang activity in high schools in 1993, 10.4 percent of black students brought a weapon to school versus 4.6 percent of whites.

I've heard people tell me it's not the black kids' fault; it's where they live and it's how they are raised. That's true, but what about when they grow up? The most ironic image to me is a gangsta daddy—not a pimp, but an actual *father* who is supposed to raise his child to be a productive person in society. I want to see today's generations doing something with their lives. I do see it but not as much as I would like. Instead, I see and hear gangsta rap. I'm not damning the music style; just the lyrics.

I want to share with you only the first verse and chorus of a song, sung by Snoop Dog called "For all my **Niggaz** and **Bitches.**"

[Verse One: Kurupt]

Well it's that slow flow, D-O-double-G, **nigga**
See these other fools but you can't see me, **nigga**
Who am I? (It's Kurupt mother**fuck**er)
Do or die (We gives a **fuck** mother**fucker**)
So slow your roll, I'm In Control like Janet
The loc-est twenty-one year old **nigga** that's on this planet
Take it for granted, if ya wanna, cuz I'm gonna
grab my strap then clear the corner, beeotch!!

[Chorus: repeat 2X]

So all my **bitches** and my **niggaz** and my **niggaz** and my **bitches**
Wave your mother**fuckin** hands in the air
And if you don't give a shit
Like we don't give a shit
Wave your mother**fuckin** fingers in the air

Do I even need to comment on that so-called music?
I know most of you remember the case of Don Imus, the white radio host who referred to the Rutgers University women's basketball team as "nappy-headed hos." After the radio show was broadcasted, Al Sharpton confronted Imus and demanded for his firing.

Days later, Imus came out with this apology:

"I want to take a moment to apologize for an insensitive and ill-conceived remark we made the other morning regarding the Rutgers women's basketball team, which lost to Tennessee in the NCAA championship game on

Tuesday. It was completely inappropriate and we can understand why people were offended. Our characterization was thoughtless and stupid, and we are sorry."

Why we have this double standard in the United States, I will never understand. Not to mention—here we go again with the apologies, as if that helped anything. Don Imus was fired and then rehired later on. Either way, the Al Sharptons and Jesse Jacksons are starting to get on my nerves, as are the people who keep using any and all racist words.

I don't know about you, but I think people like Martin Luther King Jr., who fought to liberate blacks, and Justice Thurgood Marshall (the first black justice of the Supreme Court) might be a little disappointed in some of the black generations today.

You know, I had the pleasure of vacationing in New York City over the summer with a good friend and her parents. We saw a one-man show performed by Lawrence Fishburne called *Thurgood*, in which Mr. Fishburne played the roll of Justice Thurgood, telling his story to the audience. I was never so moved by a one-man performance; without a doubt, it was unforgettable. The tragedy and struggles that Thurgood Marshall overcame are incredible, and the amount of hope that he possessed exceeds that in the black leaders of today (the Al Sharptons and Jesse Jacksons). That man was a true American who knew how to use the law to liberate blacks in America. For a man of his character to retire as the first black man on the Supreme Court, the highest court of the land, is the reason I am proud to say I am an American. Only in America can you fight against all odds and come out smiling.

At this point, I would like to share a story of my mother's with you, so that everyone gets to hear all sides of racism:

When my mother was in high school, it was mandatory to take a swimming class. Well, in a class of over thirty students, she was one of a handful of fair-skinned kids. All the girls in the class needed to get naked to take showers, and as my mother was walking, twenty black female students jumped her. They hit and beat her because she was white. Sounds backwards according to the history books, but the truth is that violence comes from both sides.

An act like that is disgusting and degrading, and yet people will try to justify it. I'll hear that whites have been committing these acts for hundreds of years and that one beating still won't make up for all the violence inflicted on blacks. When my mother lived in the Middle East, there were plenty of blacks, and they weren't any different from anyone else. Then she came to America and was beaten for the color of her skin. We cannot exonerate America for what earlier generations did to blacks, but we are new generations. We need to move forward as a people.

There is racism in this country and probably every country, and it will never go away. Hate, violence, racism, sexism, and prejudice are things that humans cannot live without. That is why world peace is impossible to attain. What we can do as a nation, however, is to make sure those people who are racist or full of hate do not make it into the highest office in the land, aren't voted into Congress, and don't wear our badges.

Chapter Eight

EMOLICIOUS

"Never date a guy who's prettier than you, or can do his make-up better than you can do your."
– Me

O H, my God, Becky look at his...eyeliner.
Okay, so that isn't exactly how the original song lyric by Sir Mixalot went, but you get the idea; the eyeliner was a little noticeable. That said, I would like to discuss the emo-fad that exploded when I was in high school. Originally, "emo" simply meant emotional, but now it symbolizes a style and type of person. For those who don't know the difference between male and female emos, let me enlighten you

Male emo: Skinny build; hair so long that his bangs fall over one or both eyes to the point where he constantly has to shake his hair off his face; wears eyeliner; wears skinny-styled pants; has writing all over his shoes; has at least a few oddly-placed piercings; writes, sings, or plays an instrument; tends to be quiet and reserved; dates girls who look like he does and can relate to his emotional side; not really big on physical fighting.

Female emo: Skinny build; long, mostly black hair that is spiky in the back; bangs that fall over one or both eyes to the point where she constantly has to shake her hair off her face; wears eyeliner; wears skinny-styled pants; has writing all over her shoes; has at least a few oddly-placed piercings; writes, sings, or plays an instrument; tends to be quiet and reserved; dates emo boys; tends to be big on physical fighting. (Believe it or not, emo girls can be tough cookies.

Not seeing much of a difference, are you? I didn't see one when I was in school, either, except for the fact that the females looked tougher. The whole point of this emolicious chapter is to explain the current fad in high school fashion, which will soon pass. I realize that some of you might fall under the category of emo, and some of you look very pretty and/or handsome with the look. My issue is the fact that the fad has somehow made self-pity acceptable. The constant self-loathing attitude I saw, and at one point participated in, is killing America. This is how I see it: When teenagers take time to self-loath, they take time away from self-achievement. They spend so much time thinking of themselves as the victims that it becomes hard to see themselves as anything else.

This theory doesn't exclude people who don't dress emo, because some people dress emo on the inside. Being emo makes life pretty easy. When you're being emo, you suck up all the pity you get from others, and it becomes an addiction. You don't have to own up to responsibility when you're too busy crying or feeling sorry for yourself. But for the people who want to become the next president, pope, senator, dance star, musician, writer, or sports star, there is no room for self-loathing.

Around the time I was a freshman, I had this huge crush on a boy I'd known since first grade. That year, we decided to secretly date. To us, that meant talking late on the phone and emailing and IM-ing each other; trust me, no one got naked when we were together. During our "relationship," we had a conversation that became an inside joke between us and, later, the thing that woke me up and ended our relationship.

I asked him what would happen if we were on a date and we

were being mugged, and he said, "I'd hold your purse and you'd fight them off." Being the silly, crush-consumed girl that I was, I ignored the warning bells in my head, the ones that told me that men were the protectors. At first, I believed he was being cute because he understood that I was one tough cookie, but when I learned that he wasn't joking, it was like a slap to the face. I broke it off and believe that it was the best choice I ever made. My point is that this current emo fad hasn't only changed the way kids dress but the way male and female roles have changed or, in this case, become the same.

The truth is, I was embarrassed that I had picked a boy who wasn't even ashamed to admit that he'd let his girlfriend fight his battles in any way, shape, or form. I never understood why males today have taken on the female role and women are starting to take on the men's role. When I say "roles," I'm not talking about jobs, like being in the military or being a fashion designer. I'm talking about attitude. When I see a man who has better hair than me and knows how to apply makeup to his own face without a mirror, I know we have a problem.

How can any of us survive if the men fight against what nature intended for them to be? If we lose men, then all we have is women, and God knows that if we ruled the world it'd be chaos. That's not to say that we've never had women who were great leaders. Women have ruled (Queen Elizabeth) fought wars (Joan of Arc) and made history. The problem I see with women running everything in life is that women are ruled by emotions (most of the time), and men rule their emotions (or at least they used to).

I don't believe it's the men who are doing this to themselves but, rather, that it's women who do it to them. Through feminism ideology, women have slammed down on the male ego by telling them they're selfish, sexist, egotistical, and—my favorite—male chauvinistic pigs. And we wonder why some men hate women. We, as women, had better watch ourselves, or sooner or later men will just become gay and the only reason we'll be needed is to populate the world, putting us right back where we started.

As I was in bed one morning, waking up from a dramatic dream, I remembered a story that my former English teacher told the class. He was walking around campus during lunch and saw two girls walking. At that same moment, he saw another girl waving at one of the pair from about twenty feet away. One of the pair ran up to her and gave her a huge hug, spinning their bodies around. The second girl in the pair looked at her other friend and just rolled her eyes in annoyance.

My teacher, being a male, thought this was pretty cold, and I have to agree, though it didn't shock any of the girls in my class. This behavior is common among girls in high school, college, business, dance clubs, and when it comes to dating. Women are the most devious, smart, cunning beings ever, until their emotions get in the way. Yes, that applies to men, too, but only to an extent. After emotions get involved, we have Britney Spears meets **Rosie** O'Donnell, and God knows that's a horrible combination.

Have you ever seen those action-thriller movies where the men just kill each other without thought—like Don Corleone, who says "It's not personal, its business"? For women it's always personal.

By this point, the girls reading this book are probably mad at me for putting down my own kind, but I can't help it; it's just so easy. On an online writers' community, I wrote short articles answering questions posed by the members of the site. One of the questions was, "Do women work harder than men?" My answer: yes. I'd like to share the article with you, but before I do I want to clarify something. I realize that we are young, and most of us aren't married or consider ourselves to be "women," but one day we will be. One day, we have to grow into woman who we can be proud of.

The article:

Women do work harder than men, not because they have to, but because they want to. People work because they need to purchase provisions to survive, not because they like to work, and yet we still have women who dive into the workplace because they feel that they have to prove something. Yes, there are some people out there who love to work, who have to be doing something, but they are in a position where that is possible. I'm not talking about single people, couples with no kids, or even parents with grown children. I'm talking about married or single women whose kids need their care and attention, but who choose to give that time up with their kids to work.

The United States has come a long way concerning the equality of women in the workforce, in political stances, and as people as a whole. Women who have working husbands, who have kids, and who have everything they need but still feel they need to work are getting themselves into a world of hurt. I know a woman who is kind beyond words but creates problems for herself by trying to fit thirty-six hours into a twenty-four hour day. The woman I know tries to save the world, but she doesn't know how to tell her kids no. I know it stresses her husband out; you can see it in his eyes, the way he stands, or the way he crosses his arms. The actions of this woman, no matter how noble, put a strain on her marriage and on the children's lives.

I can't understand why a person, woman or man, would rather work when unnecessary versus stay home and work at building her/his home life. Never doubt that being a stay-at-home parent is a job, because it is the hardest job one can have. I took a class in child development, and what

I heard the most is that there are angry parents. There was a story of a woman who leaves her child at a daycare all day, not because she has to but because she chooses to work so she can say she's a career woman. Then that child doesn't want to come home with her at the end of the day. That woman has no reason to be angry with the care provider, her child, or her husband; it's purely her fault. Her child has become attached to the caregiver because babies look for love, and if their mothers don't give it to them, they look for new "mothers." This woman has just created more work for herself. I am not in any way, shape, or form saying that there aren't mothers who need to work; there are. I just ask that you be all you can be.

Be all you can be as a woman, a mother, and a wife who makes sure dinners are on the table, hugs her children, and greets her husband with a kiss and a promise.

Essh, that's a lot to think about, but the reality of things is that those responsibilities have already hit some of us. Don't be discouraged, though—there is always time to make life better, to change your future, and to be the best you can be. If you are in a situation where you are a mother or father and haven't even graduated high school yet, don't feel alone. If you drown yourself in drugs to feel more alive, you are not alone. You are not your drugs. There is nothing you can't do, and don't let anyone tell you differently. People who are always trying to push you down, who never smile and think only of themselves, are negative people. You need to get away from negative people and become a positive person.

If young girls give the impression to boys that they want them to be sensitive, then guys will be encouraged to be feminine. Everything in life has a snowball affect. If we tell young boys that being girly is fine, then they will grow up to be feminine men.

Then those men will be easily pushed around by the women who were raised to think that girls are meant to be tough like old-fashioned men. Then the roles in a typical household are turned upside down. There has to be balance in life. There is a time and place for everything, including how men and women should act. I like for men to be men and women to be women. They don't have to be stereotypical—just natural. We are where we are because of the snowball effect of our past societies. Even something so simple as attitude can change the whole world, for better or worse. I'd hate to start a new snowball affect that will one day destroy the world.

AFTERWORD

To everyone who wrote in: You are going places. The ability to think freely is the key to achieving anything. It amazed me that out of the hundreds of people that knew about the book, only the few who wrote in were willing to make a difference in their world. This is not a cause for depression but, rather, a motivation for realization and triumph. It always seems that it takes a great few to make a difference.

I hope that through this short, sweet, and very blunt book you were able to see things from a different perspective and maybe even learn a few things.

I don't have a degree from Harvard and I can't dance the tango, but I can see when my country needs some help. I'm a concerned youth who wants answers and solutions, not babble and more nonsense. I'm taking a stand with my words and actions, and I will not back down or be afraid. I'll fight for my country because, when the time comes, I know she'll fight for me.

Before I go, I'd like you to meet Marlee, a thirteen-year-old girl who doesn't feel very safe in our world.

> "The world is horrible. We've polluted it and stained it with our sin. We're racist and not just white people, black people, too. We're sexist; we're extremely rude to the homosexual part of the nations. We treat the media as our

lords and masters. I don't think it will ever get much better. I don't think we'll have time, unless we really change. Otherwise the world is going to die because people can't figure out how to live with it. But we'd have to change quickly. With the way people are nowadays, that may never happen. And kids don't feel like we can do anything. We've been undermined for centuries. So what are we supposed to do? No one wants to listen to us. They'd rather listen to somebody who might as well be a zombie. I don't want it to be like this. Most people don't. We want peace and a clean Earth and lots of good, nice things. They just don't seem to come. Maybe, just maybe, when this generation gets older, maybe we'll turn the world around."

- Marlee Dommer, 13, Michigan

Marlee is counting on the future generations of America to make the world a better place—let's not let her down.

THE END

For now.

Thanks, cheers, and many more years to come...

There are so many people to thank and so little space on this page to do it. I would like to thank God for sticking with me through the hectic rush, long afternoons, and doubting times. I would like to thank my parents for believing in me enough to invest in this book and for sticking up for me when I didn't deserve it.

To Rick Roberts, a man daring enough to let me talk freely on his radio show. Without you, this book would still be on my computer hard drive taking up space.

To my editor Katie at Legacy Editorial Consulting, who was willing to work with me. She helped me turn my clutter of thoughts into coherent literature that I'm eager to show off. Thank you, Katie; I would never have been able to put it all together without your guidance.

There is only one guy I know that will spend an hour on the phone with me and let me ramble about the first thing that pops in to my head: my older brother Michael. Thank you for all the hours I spent racking up your cell phone bill, and thank you for letting me share your stories with others.

To my crazy best friend who took her sweet time writing something for the book but who never disappoints me. Shannon, you are my very best friend, sister in my heart, and a thorn in my side when it comes to politics—but you're the smartest liberal I know. To another decade of friendship, cheers!

I would like to thank the man who handed me a Robert B. Parker novel the end of my sophomore year in high school and showed me a world where only fiction can take you. Thank you, Mr. Thompson without you I wouldn't even know how to type two sentences together.

I believe thanks are in order to the very famous MySpace—without the place for spaces I wouldn't have been able to contact the people I did. Thanks, Tom, and creators of MySpace.

To everyone who submitted their comments and poems: You are the future and the strength that will help America survive. Thank you.